VROOM!
HOW A CAR ENGINE WORKS FOR KIDS

BABY PROFESSOR

EDUCATION KIDS

Speedy Publishing LLC
40 E. Main St. #1156
Newark, DE 19711
www.speedypublishing.com

Copyright 2016

Starting a car is as simple as turning a key. But have you ever wondered what really happens? Every car has an engine below the hood.

An engine is a machine that uses many different parts to convert fuel into energy, or power. An engine creates enough power to make the car move.

Just like your body converts food into energy to move, a car engine converts gasoline into motion. Some newer cars, known as hybrids, also use electricity from batteries. Some get energy from the sun, using solar panels.

When your body needs fuel, you feed it food. When your car needs fuel, you "feed" it gasoline. The process of converting gasoline into power is called "internal combustion".

Internal combustion engines use tiny and controlled explosions to generate the power. It is needed to move your car. A car engine creates explosions hundreds of times per minute.

CAMSHAFT

CAM

MIXTURE IN

INTAKE VALVE

COMBUSTION CHAMBER

CYLINDER BLOCK

CONNECTING ROD

CRANKSHAFT

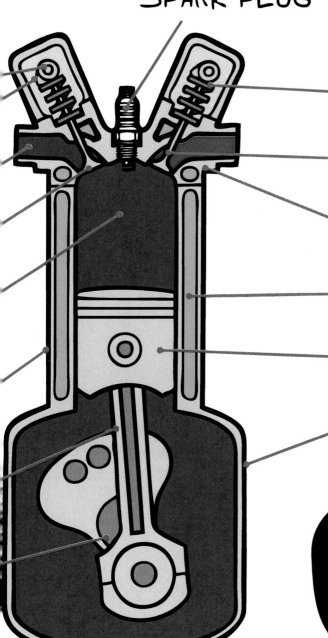

SPARK PLUG

VALVE SPRING

EXHAUST VALVE

CYLINDER HADE

COOLING WATER

PISTON

CRANKCASE

INTERNAL COMBUSTION ENGINE

The engine then takes the energy released and uses it to power your car.

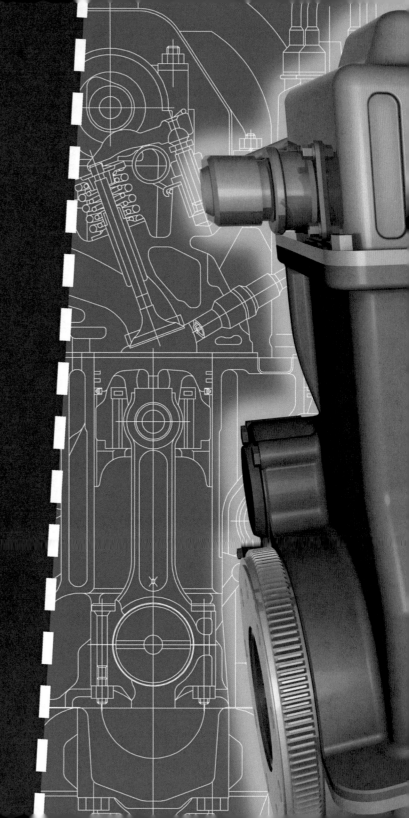

The explosions forces pistons in the engine to move. When the energy from the first explosion has used up, a new explosion occurs. This powers the pistons to move continuously until it becomes a cycle giving the car the power needed to run.

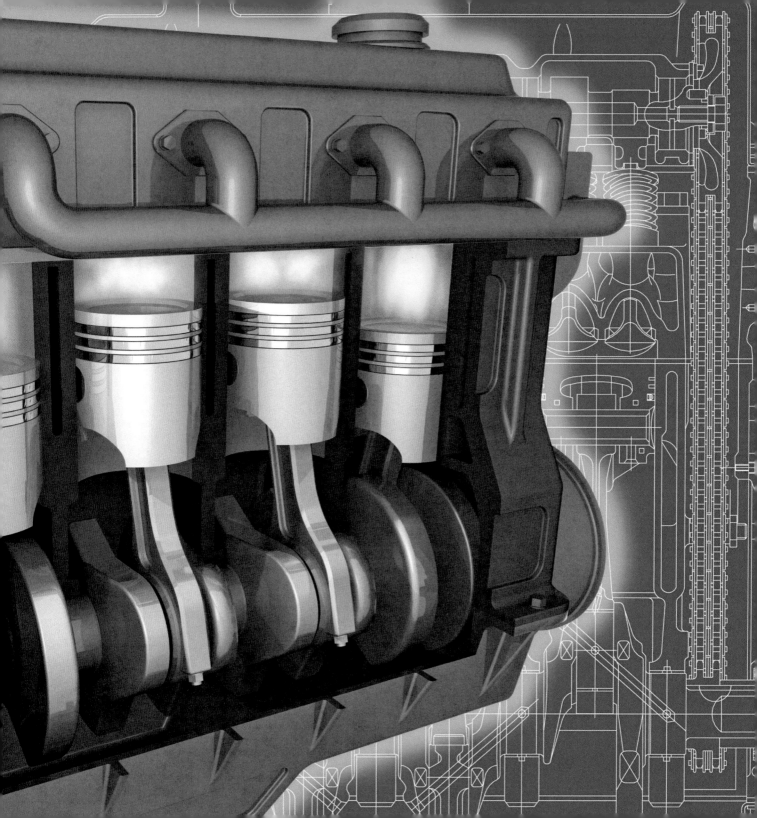

A car engine is a very efficient machine. It burns fuel in containers, which are closed. It holds a major part of the heat energy released by the fuel, and turns it into mechanical energy that drives the car along.

Here are main parts of a car engine.

Cylinders – They are made of super-strong metal and locked, but they open and close like bicycle pumps: they have tight-fitting pistons that can slide up and down inside them.

They are built around a set of "cooking pots". The fuel burns inside the cylinders.

Pistons — are small parts inside the cylinders. The piston's function is to move up and down. By making this movement, the piston pulls a mixture of gasoline and air into the cylinder and then compress it back up toward the spark plug.

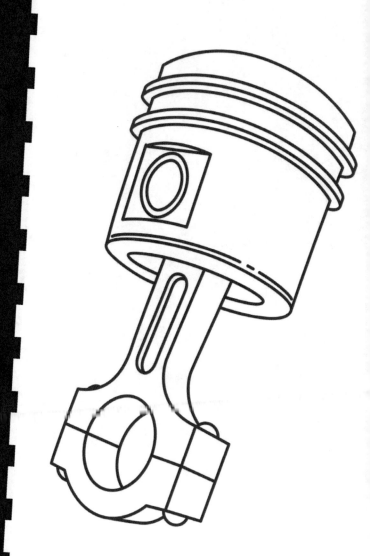

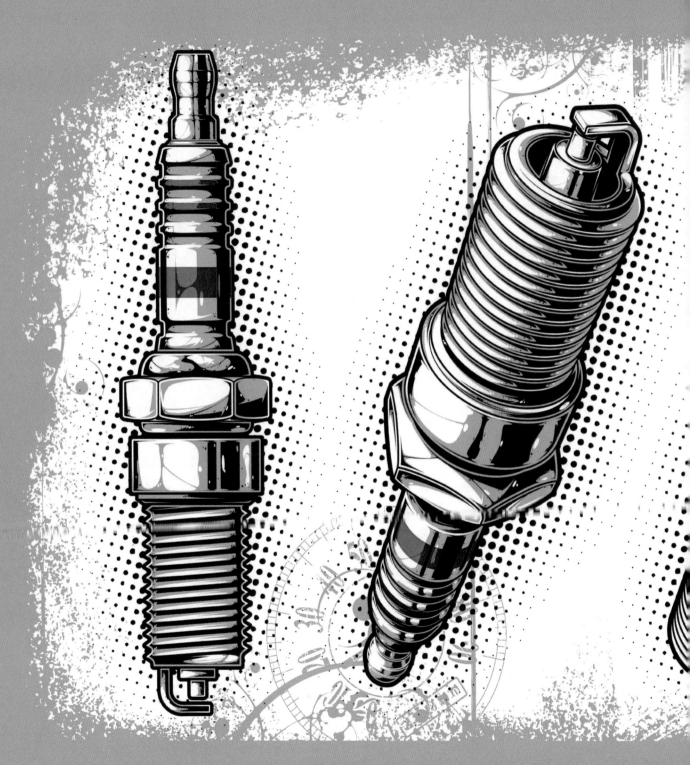

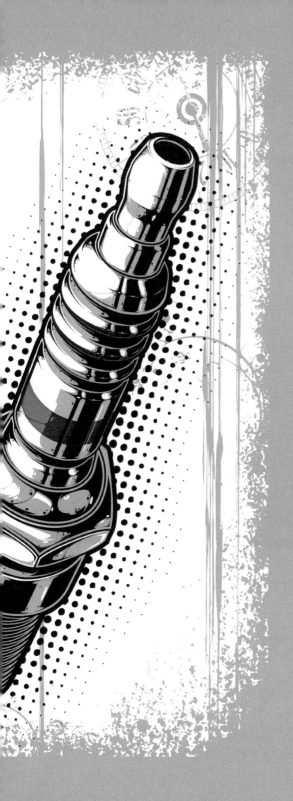

Spark Plug – The spark plug's function is an electrically controlled device that makes a spark to set fire to the fuel. The resulting explosion creates energy which the engine uses to power the car.

Inlet Valve - It allows a mixture of fuel and air to enter the cylinder from a carburetor or electronic fuel-injector.

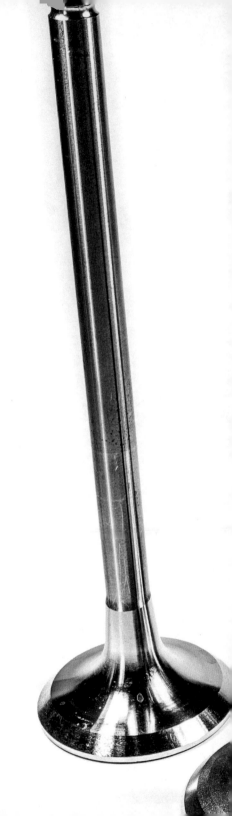

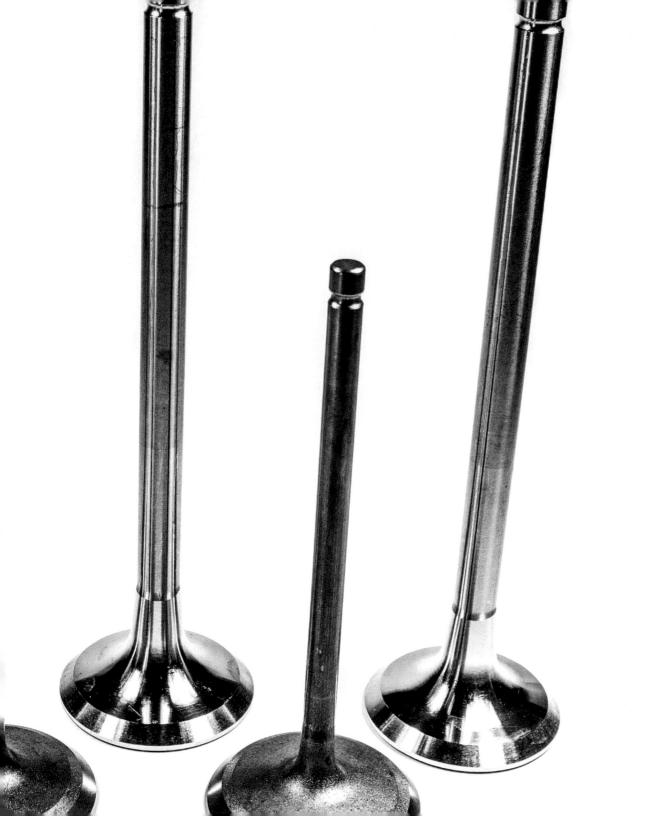

Outlet valve- lets the exhaust gases escape.

The flywheel is a large heavy metal disc that is attached to the crankshaft. The fly wheel aids the engine to keep running smoothly. It has teeth that moves by the motor.

A crankshaft gives and takes energy to many parts of the engine. It moves back and forth as the wheel rotates. The crankshaft is attached to the pistons.

The exhaust gas
pertains to the
gas released
from this entire
process. It is from
the combustion
of fuels like oil,
natural and diesel.
In cars, they are
the gases that
engines give out.

The Engine Cooling System functions by controlling the heat in the car engine. Water is pumped into the passage around the cylinders and then through the radiators to cool down. It prevents the overheating or even burning of your car's engine.

Oil greases parts of the engine to allow a smooth movement. Oil is pumped out of a pan that gets rid of dirt. Oil also affects the life of your car's engine.

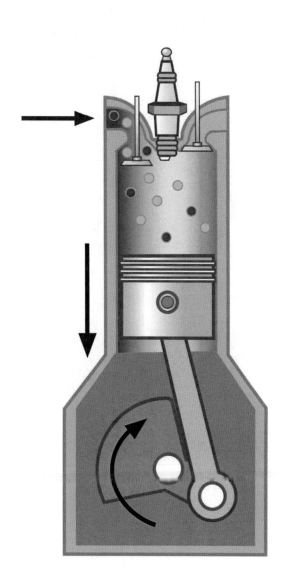
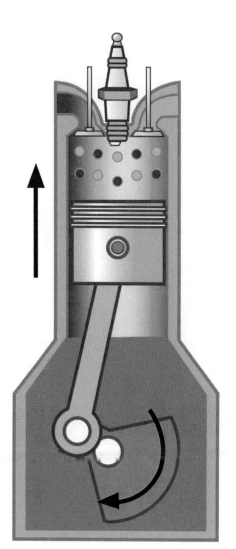
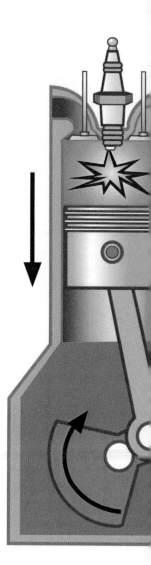

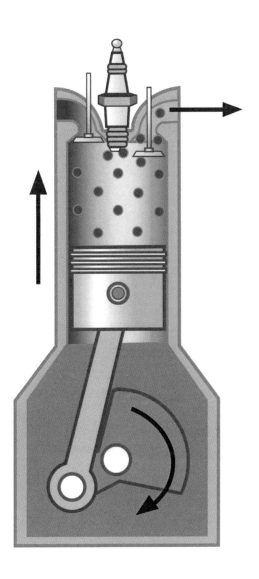

The process of making power in a car engine is an endless repetition. The car works with a four-stroke engine. The strokes are repeated over and over, generating power.

The four strokes of the engine refer to intake, compression, combustion, and exhaust. Let's take a closer look at what happens during each phase.

FOUR

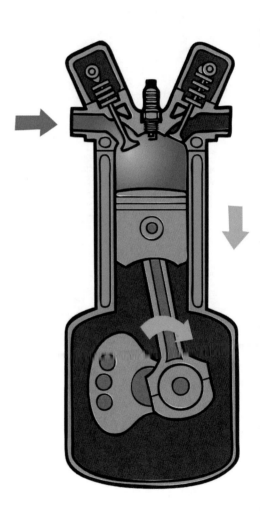

INTAKE

TROKE CYCLE ENGINE

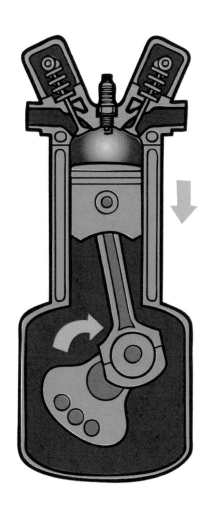

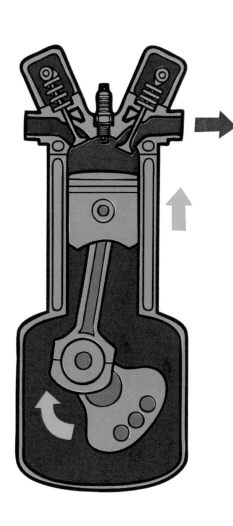

PRESSION   COMBUSTION   EXHAUST

FOUR STROKE ENGINE

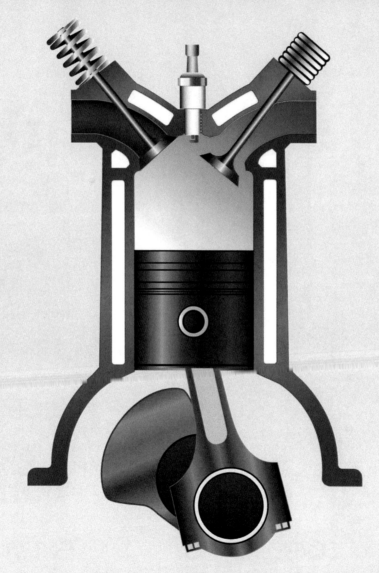

INTAKE

Intake- In the intake cycle, the intake valve opens, and the piston moves down. This begins the cycle by leading air and gas into the engine.

Compression- As the compression cycle begins, the piston moves up and pushes the air and gas into a smaller space, compressing the mixture. A smaller space means a more powerful explosion.

COMPRESSION

FOUR STROKE ENGINE

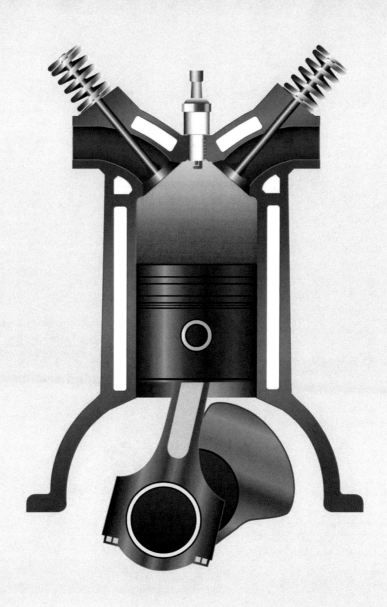

FOUR STROKE ENGINE

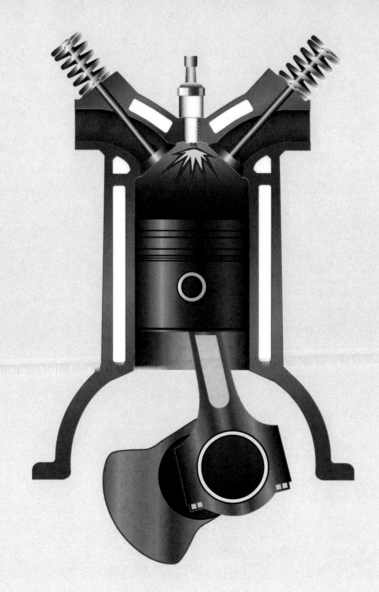

COMBUSTION

Combustion –the spark plug makes a spark that ignites and explodes the gas. The power of the explosion forces the piston back down.

Exhaust-through the last part of the cycle, the exhaust valve opens to release waste gas created by the explosion. This gas is moved to a converter, where it is cleaned, and then through the muffler before it exits the vehicle through the tailpipe.

EXHAUST

FOUR STROKE ENGINE

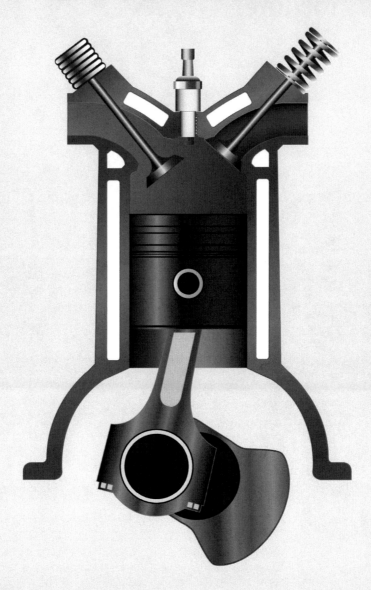

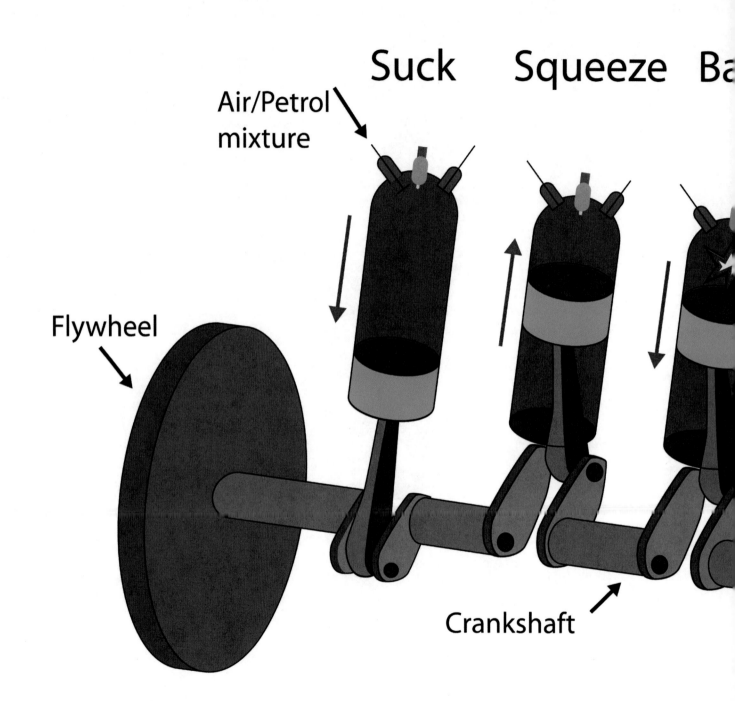

Blow

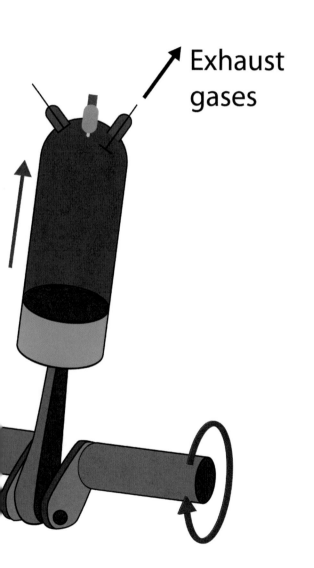

Exhaust gases

The whole cycle
then repeats itself,
and with each
repetition the car
carries you closer
to your destination.

Did you know that cars have more than just one piston and valve? If you have more pistons, your car probably is powerful.

Did you know that the world's first automobile was used by the French Army? It was steamed-powered and self-propelled. It was used to move cannons.

Visit

BABY PROFESSOR
EDUCATION KIDS

www.BabyProfessorBooks.com

to download Free Baby Professor eBooks
and view our catalog of new and exciting
Children's Books

Made in the USA
Monee, IL
07 August 2024

63369711R00038